from the east

RENARD PRESS LTD

124 City Road
London EC1V 2NX
United Kingdom
info@renardpress.com
020 8050 2928

www.renardpress.com

From the East first published by Renard Press Ltd in 2024

Text © John Greening, 2024

Cover design by Will Dady

Printed and bound in the UK on carbon-balanced papers by CMP Books

ISBN: 978-1-80447-109-8

9 8 7 6 5 4 3 2 1

John Greening asserts his moral right to be identified as the author of this work in accordance with the Copyright, Designs and Patents Act 1988.

CLIMATE POSITIVE Renard Press is proud to be a climate positive publisher, removing more carbon from the air than we emit and planting a small forest. For more information see renardpress.com/eco.

All rights reserved. This publication may not be reproduced, stored in a retrieval system or transmitted, in any form or by any means – electronic, mechanical, photocopying, recording or otherwise – without the prior permission of the publisher.

From the East

60 Huntingdonshire Codices

JOHN GREENING

RENARD PRESS

author's note

In his excellent book, *Poetry*, David Constantine asks, 'Why should a *local* habitation interest anyone but the locals?' Answering his own question, he explains how a poet must 'convert the personal, anecdotal, and accidental into the figurative' and find the 'allegory' of their life. This is essentially what I have been doing since the late 1980s, when I began writing thirty-two 'Huntingdonshire Eclogues' (published later in *Fotheringhay and Other Poems*), about day-to-day life in a county which had ceased to exist in 1974. These were unusually long-lined poems, all in tercets, each one just fitting on a page, composed in a kind of loose hexameter. The form owed much to the new freedom offered up by an Amstrad word processor. They were followed ten years later by 'Huntingdonshire Nocturnes' (*The Home Key*, 2003), more of a summer sequence, chiefly lit by moon and stars. This time there were forty-two poems in tercets, but of different lengths, more tautly composed with a six-beat line (still unrhymed). Another decade on, with the publication of *Hunts: Poems 1979–2009*, I wanted to bring the sequences together by adding a shorter group of new, rather autumnal 'Huntingdonshire Elegies', now introducing some rhyme. That seemed to be that. But then – before the pandemic – what looked like a trilogy became a *Huntingdonshire Quartet*. My 'Codices' were begun during a walk on Boxing Day in

2017, and continued to emerge as the 'Beast from the East' prowled the land. That wintriness is evident here. The 64th poem was composed on my 64th birthday in March (I later removed four). They are all of fifteen lines, loyal as ever to the tercet, and that long six-beat line remains, but now I am using a regular (if not always full) rhyme. Why 'Codices'? Perhaps because I am being more than usually literary. Winter, after all, is a time to hunker down and read.

JOHN GREENING
March 2024, Stonely

from the east

for Katie and Rosie

I

Following power lines, three of them, insulators
like gleaming mini angels, a trio of undecorated
Christmas trees, brown, on poles as upright as

memorial crosses. Boxing Day. The hunt is ready
to pass under the wires, but at this hour nobody
hails my shadow stretching itself across a muddy

sown field beside that single cottage, where once
an old woman offered a smile. Following lines,
their gifts of light and heat, to a chain-link fence

around the gas pumping station: the North Sea
cries Stop. Let the powerful march and be
hailed by a singing distant host in white. My energy

reserves are not so great. I turn to face the future
where I've come from: and it's wireless. Human nature
finds its way, king or shepherd, poet or teacher.

2

'Who made the eyes?' The question Herbert put
in God's mouth, whether expecting an answer or not,
before we looked down at the web in our hands and were caught.

We know a man who'd know, perhaps, who lives with a maze
on the misty edge of vision. Has he threaded the eyes'
mysterious centre? He would offer the name of a disease

for you to Google. I, says Nature. I, says God,
and Herbert up at Leighton says he has seen weird
visions over Little Gidding. A sky of blood.

A cloud like a cross. Just make sure you look
at what's there under your nose. Famous for its lack
of any sight worth seeing, yet a walk

over this airfield to study the light on the new furrows,
the bars of brightness through hawthorn, the drifting arrows
of geese, the needlepoint turbines, has its glories.

3

That stone again, *London 62 Miles,*
reminds me of the Huntingdonshire man for whom it spells
Samarkand, who drove a cartload of Brussels

down the main road once, then back to plough
his old furrow. What does London know?
And why should a man not be tired of it by now?

No, Johnson, you keep out of this. That stone
on the B645 has more to tell us than
your dictionary, which I refute thus. Have done

with capitals, and think of the lower case out here
where garden, friends, TV and family are fair
exchange for all that vanity. Park the car,

unlock the door. Yes, things could be worse,
unaccommodated, or all these years of verse
ending at a stone like his, a ploughman following a horse.

4

Stand well clear. I open a colourful box
from the last English manufacturer of fireworks,
famous from Hong Kong to the 2012 Olympics.

How long and slow a fuse it is that stretches back
to those unmarked sheds beyond our hedge: a crack,
a swish, a fizz, a daylight air attack…

It's only the creator testing his wares. One night
I walked home through the dark just as they shot
(for promotional purposes) the Reverend with his arms out-

stretched in front of a Catherine wheel. From time to time
our sleeps are disturbed, but not by what should set them
spinning, a fuse that burns on up into the home

of Guy Fawkes's onomatopoeic judge,
John Popham: that I could so zealously urge
our children — make a guy, a bonfire, fit for your age.

5

His cottage somewhere the other side of the main line
waits for you to make your crossing. Let a train
go suthering by before you follow its sign

through snub oaks and balks. One legendary
day after the war, you recall, Edmund Blunden
opened a cupboard and all the poems escaped to London

with a passing roar of approval. Now, here's a 'centre'
on the fen edge, where geology shifts, and to encounter
a mouldywarp or a starnel you need only enter

the living room, the study, leave the known language,
walk in the garden, write beneath a greengage,
lay in the dovecote your *oo-* and *ah-* and *o*-gauge

lines about your multi-storey life, how friends
forsake you, how such straight and clear and simple minds
inspire you, ere the mad red barrier descends.

6

'May your shelves always overflow with books' –
the framed poster, ghost of a Christmas present, looks
at home there among those three thousand backs

turned on me tonight as I sit writing. *Aren't
there enough of us?* they seem to ask. A faint
disturbance at the end of the field, look. Traffic can't

get through – our winterbourne has usurped the road:
we walk around and find a homeowner stood
cheerfully telling stories about the water, the flood

that always comes when you least expect it, like poetry,
how everyone rushes to seal their vulnerability
and keep it out. He has electricity

and his only book is safe. Lights flash, the cars
continue their plunge, carried away: one steers
hopelessly, stalls, gets stuck on this stretch of verse.

7

Time to change the month-old suspension in the jar,
that mini monolith, a sodden souvenir
of the Bronze Age, from Flag Fen, Peterborough.

Eleven years I've seen its three millennia preserved
in Anglian water, with their pale certificate of proof,
time waster or charging point, balanced above

a smiling mother and baby, a stone arrowhead,
a Royal Air Force cap and a commemorative plate,
at the right hand of the Mission speaker it has tried

to emulate with music of prehistory, the Fen
Country's wind and sky and sorrow scored for Then,
performed by Now: a ceremonial march between

dead trees. Time to put on *Tapiola*, watch
the silver birch I bought from Woolworths begin to stretch
to its reopening sale, catkins lash and switch.

8

Step by step, tentatively towards the bridge,
ice on the lane, sheets of ice, walk on the verge,
walk on the gravel, careful not to slide and lurch

into the dark river, half frozen, but running high,
its message scrawled at our feet and on the handrails in dry
grass or reed. From the fields comes the wink of an eye

to any so old they still recall how you would find
your blades on such a morning and be out. But your mind
is running on how you'll start the car; the future is signed

No Skating and points to the city. There goes
a motorcyclist, warily; all in leathers, the crows
wheel across in mockery. A solitary child, who's

been left to stand at the door while the windscreen is de-iced
part-waves at us. And Mr Noon, who's passed
us once, arrives again, hugging the *Guardian* to his chest.

9

Each year grows colder on the earth,
the Renaissance thinkers thought as they grew further
from Eden and the Fall. So Cromwell put his faith

in a high-speed skating route out of Huntingdon
and let his Ironsides lead the country on
to where an icy commonwealth could freeze the sun.

But they were wrong. We've seen the temperature rise
and zero put in doubt with our own eyes,
the Arctic thaw set in. Yet listen to the news

that follows the breaking ice – of how a steely cold
returns, as it always must, that unrelenting hold.
The wall's down, true, unloved, as Frost foretold,

but was he blinded by his memory, by the day,
forgetful of his own winter night, the way
a seed shoots, an old man's books decay?

10

Where did he bury it, old Mr Pepys?
What cipher conceals its location? You drive to the shops
passing his farmhouse. The windscreen wiper wipes

the water meadows. On this side, gravel pits,
hospital, school; on that, the invisible Ouse waits
with its own meandering tale, a goose feather notes

a change in weather, and somewhere near the pub or church
you may spot one who's visiting, just to search
for that precious hoard of ordinary life. February, March…

now who keeps a diary? A month, a year goes past
unremarked, except for your blogs and brags, those post-
horns to the world, but what you're thinking… cyber-mist

conceals it, all that's left of the mystery, the moving river,
impossible to dig up, wound in its ever-
tangling skeins of you, until the record's over.

II

After so many winters, you find you have trodden
your name into the snow. It is marked in brown, sodden
patches of grass, an angel, a doughnut: the years harden

to an icy grey around you, but there is your name,
unmissable. Except others are doing the same
on playing fields and patios. When it snows, I'm

the big noise, not the silent snowman with coal
for eyes and carrot for a nose; but when it thaws, what fool
mistook such vegetable jewels for a soul?

After so many winters with a mind of talc and glass
your name is dead grass, a few patches of whiteness
and traces of a handprint. When Spring is witness

to the unveiling of statues in Whitehall or in St Ives,
it's you and I will have to choose who serves
a life sentence in history; who it is survives.

12

Compline. Vigils. Lauds. Out to the wind and ice
along the Easton Road, where Todd's Cottage prays
for better broadband speeds, a monk of the Priory goes

in the name of Augustine of Hippo, slowly, slowly,
up the hill, thinking of Africa, the Vandals, the Early
Church and how it found its way out of the folly

of Manichaeism. The sun is rising over the Fens
beyond that ridge, where creatures live among the dense
reedbeds that would like to invade their morning devotions,

breathing eth and thorn into their Latin pieties.
But this moment is where the God of England is
among these kneeling men. The plain voice of praise

rings above caravans, and the skeleton of a barn
they burnt the other week. The monastery is gone
except, occasionally, in the field you'll find a painted stone.

13

Poetry, history, Greek, *Where Angels Fear to Tread,*
balanced precariously, hoping to be read,
but we're working through boxed sets, watching the dead

pile up in *Happy Valley.* Look, a scene
in the cemetery where Sylvia Plath is buried. There's rain
in Heptonstall, like here. Why have the Hugheses been

so often in the corner of our living room? That thrush would know,
cracking snailmail open, and so would the crow
that keeps on following us. At Newnham, let's park below

the window of her old room. Had it all survived
would they have sat into their sixties, well behaved
as us to watch such dramas? Hard to imagine. Yet we've

come through our forty episodes of noir, and played
at hunting for the ruby in the mine. Pass me the guide.
Or as we used to say: what's on the other side?

14

A printed book, and when it goes out of print, still
the digital file exists. Is that what it's like, all
physical evidence of existence gone, yet there in the file

of invisible things… I gave our neighbour a copy of *Threading
a Dream*, my Egypt memoir, which apparently he was reading
before he died. His son is out in the wintry garden

to burn what's left of a gardening life, one
of few words, those he left to his wife, and none
were finally available to her. They used to enjoy the sound

of our daughter's piano, they said, for which we blessed them both
and remembered our first ever flat. Always beneath
that mattress, the listening ear; here, it's hearth to hearth

in this old terrace, though books help make it soundproof.
'More books than's good for it,' our landlady used to huff
as she read the *Morning Star* inside the *Telegraph*.

15

My friend from Mainz, home of Gutenberg, has written
asking when we'll come. That familiar pattern
of his hand, so very German; he still loves Britain,

or what he thinks we are. It might well appear
we're trapped in a living chunk of *Aufklärung* here
(though light didn't come until the war's final year).

I told his children there would be unicorns in the park
(*Einhorn* for *Eichhorn*) when they stayed with us, way back.
Vanbrugh façade, Adam gatehouse. Such a stack

of reading since he took me first to that famous press,
or taught me how GDR editions would cost less,
and sorted the word order, the world order, yes.

We'll visit soon, old friend, to marvel at each spine
precisely in its place, and compare them with how mine
are heaped and dropped and bent; pour me some Hessen wine.

16

Those dark things, the spidery ganglions, are mistletoe:
you wonder who owns the tree, whether they know
what they're conjuring, if they've heard of the infamous throw

that killed the most popular god – such an innocent sprig
couldn't possibly carry a warhead, go ballistic
or threaten hearts of oak. The danger of thinking big,

when here are a thousand thousand rich little kisses,
tactical and tactile enough to divert any crisis
from Northern Rock to Ragnarok. The myth of Croesus,

not Baldur, comes to mind. Like money, this parasite
locks itself in the big apple and holds on tight
to the common lime. But nobody can reach it. No rite

is under way to mark the start of a new era
or restoration of the old. Perhaps people fear
collapse – or the spirit of the Commonwealth is still potent here?

17

My gift at Christmas forty years ago: *The Cantos*
of Ezra Pound, a bright red brick of boundless
genius to hurl through Betjeman's windows

from my parents' house. I take them off the shelves –
or 'it', since the poems don't incline to present themselves
discretely, but as a blister pack, whose character dissolves

in his own acid. 'Regard them as a quarry.'
But now I can only see a grinding heavy lorry
spread its dust across the hedges; then a weary

explosives expert hold a cheap and useless Pound
Shop power tool. From Rapallo, the hollow sound
of meaning being crushed until there's simply a profound

air of nothingness, a sad and soulless look.
And you can see it now, the fatal line, the crack
where all the blackshirts march and sing. I close the book.

18

Typing up on the top floor of the Tudor castle
I used to teach in, typing pages of old verse
for some collection I dreamt of, trying to pass

the late evening shift's long final hour,
typing on a better computer than mine, hoping to store
the text on its hard drive. One page more

of the dozens: it's a sestina, 'For the Six Wives',
elaborate piece of artifice compressing their lives
into six verses (and an envoi). No one believes

this place where she died is really haunted, but typing away
I reached the passage where I'd written about the day
of Catherine's funeral, how Anne Boleyn… and, as I say,

there are no ghosts. But at the line, the word, 'Anne',
the computer crashed. I typed it again. It crashed, and then
the poem simply vanished. I exited. I ran.

19

The Kimbolton Hoard is on display in St Neots Museum,
though they won't say where it was found. There's a rumour
it was somewhere in that field beside the alpaca farm.

The metal detectors will be out. As to why it was buried…
you might well do the same if you were worried
someone was after your money. Then there was that story:

the guy who invested a small amount in Bitcoin, but forgot
and put his hard drive in the bin, along with – what?
seventy million or so? Zeros mark the spot

at the local landfill. Not exactly a sacrifice,
though maybe in the Iron Age it was the price
of health or happiness, a way to keep the peace.

In two thousand years, when they at last dredge
that small box out of the earth, the museum can stage
an exhibition of life in the Alpaca Age.

20

Talking of Fake News, there was that manuscript by Donne,
an autograph copy, it was said, the one
found in the stables of Kimbolton Castle: they put it on

the front page of the *TLS*. It was possible.
He might well have passed through here to Keyston, or to call
on local poets. If so, it's a minor miracle –

'Good Friday… Riding Westward' in his own hand –
perhaps a copy he brought with him, and left behind
for the Duke to read, or Sir John; or simply (absent-minded)

dropped as he climbed on to his horse to continue west
towards his place in literature. A kind of test
of the true Metaphysical: who can be last

to survive outside his own holograph? It's his word
against the experts'. Death, proud as ever, heard
the news and God went on battering, undeterred.

21

Holly, given us by a man who loved where he lived,
prickly, too, if you disagreed with what he believed.
Holm, he said, Hulver. Ensure your hand is gloved.

And once it's in your head, expect anxious birds
to strip its redness, its high definition. Holly wood's
ideal for print, he said, will keep your exact words

without blurring them, will totally respect your view
as its screen grows wider, surrounding all you do
with the glossy sound of carolling. As if he knew

this scratched request would come, appointing me to ghost
and script the whole story. Out there, the cast
of Druids, Romans, Christians, made up, dressed

with whip and mail and blood. In here, the poet's work
of rescuing in a few short hours, on a scroll of bark
in *opegrapha scripta*, those berries from the dark.

22

As Madeleine Albright's brooches ('Read My Pins')
were how she'd convey her mood, the approach, what chance
success (a good day was a flower, a bad – with puns

intended for listening Russians – a bug), so maybe these
from Peterborough had meanings too, though smashed with praise
into the bog instead of spotlit under glass.

Tribes came paddling through the Fens, no doubt,
as Ms Albright did by Boeing to negotiate
with terrorist or despot. It is a long-haul flight

from the Bronze Age, but they had their special pins
to intimidate or to placate; and expensive weapons
out of sight, but ready to deploy. Now she opens

the talks as if a thousand years were a single breath
on which she has flown by eagle, honey bee or moth
and brings a torch, a caduceus, good faith.

23

A red kite hovering over my books cries
it wants to be well read, fit for the skies'
hall of learning, asks to be thrown something wise

to digest, not quick to grasp, but to occupy its wheeling
mind in this wintry half-light. What is appealing
to one familiar already, surely, with Shakespeare's mewling

hellkite and the daughters of Lear, with Hopkins, Hughes…?
I'd skim it a slim contemporary volume so it could choose,
but the fork of the tail dismisses what it already knows –

ruler of air and earth, back from the edge of extinction,
who now controls the surveillance of a county of no distinction –
as old news. *H is for Hawk*, perhaps? Or fiction,

philosophy, theology – something to appease this restless soul
at my study window. Drone-like presences roll
around the satellite dish; their hungry, demented call.

24

I wonder whether my spitting image is still on retreat
in Wales, Gregynog, that laboratory of the spirit
where I saw him once, a strange encounter. A private

press goes stamp-stamp and, look… here's my card,
Magic for Children, stuffed in a drawer. How weird
to see yourself appear to yourself as I then appeared.

And that was me too on the platform at Sevenoaks
with Dad (just like your father, everyone jokes)
carrying a printing press in a huge cardboard box,

with type and smelly ink and sticky rollers, all
ready to go once we got it home, a mechanical
mystery, the mystery being *why*. Let me call

that number on the magic card, or my father's name,
or Google all the records for the day I became
another face… the answer is always just the same.

25

Redgrove's birthday. The gulls now leave the household tip
and pass in formation over Falmouth: a galloping shape
to which they cry *grimoire, grimoire*. Our nearest ship

is probably a pub: it's hard to get much further
from the sea than my study ('in a season of calm weather'),
though they say it could come if the level rises just another

inch or two above the Fens. Imagine that wave,
like a Peter Redgrove poem. Formidable. You have to believe
you can take it on, rise to the occasion, reading, dive

into the boozy foam. Storms there tonight,
first of the year, Maenporth Beach battered to a white
noise of mud and jazz and legend. I sit and write

inland here, quietly, the rain beating its restrained
counterpoint on our double glazing. There's something of a wind,
but nothing to stir the roots. Elsewhere, Redgrove's mind.

26

Greek books spread over the dining-room table,
the cat pawing futilely at the page, unable
to get further than *mew*. And you: the intolerable

struggle with the optative, your personal Thermopylae,
armed with a spartan flatbread. You sit there happily
from dawn confronting voices and dialects, and would probably

continue through to dusk. What is twilight in Greek?
You've pinned vocabulary round the house (*water, chalk*)
though it's Greek to me. Now and again I hear you speak

a phrase from Herodotus or a snatch of pastoral verse,
and think how poets would have been expected to possess
such knowledge once. In the grammatical immerse

and scorn the tempest, then, swim the wine-dark world,
your temperate flag from the Aegean unfurled
beside our pond each Eos, in St Neots cold.

27

A gap leads through to where the allotments were.
No sign of them except our neighbour's strip, where
it extends out into the field. It was there

his Dad would walk a plough. Sunflowers tip
towards autumn, maize brightens, the *pip-pip*
of silver hubcaps tries to fool the birds as I slip

through to read the river's latest. I could say:
remember this before it was improved, back in the day
when the nightsoil was collected from the very place

where I write, the old terraces' back door then
being the front? Instead we pass, wave, pretend
we can't hear the tractor approaching the field end,

snaking its way around his vegetable love,
on this occasion prepared to let things be, to leave
his allotment of past pleasures, to take and to give.

28

A life held together by little rituals: choosing
foam or gel; wetting the razor, and wondering whose
bleary face this is in the small round glass.

Preparing the cafetière with two portions decaf
to one of the real thing, anticipating the safe
landing of toast on plate. Spread the Flora. Enough

jam to keep the diet quiet. Turf the cat
from your chair as you do your balancing act to where you've sat
for thirty years to have this breakfast. No chat,

as that would be uncivilised, though returning
from her morning walk, Jane tells me it's raining.
Radio 4. I try to mute the Business, burning

my mouth with coffee, spilling it (and jam) on the Sports
page as the cat prepares to jump up. Now, Thought
for the Day: my bloody blood pressure tablets. Abort.

29

Brexit was not what the thing in my study said,
but disillusioned with the heron and the grass snake, in dread
of the green bottle, it left the pond. Bufo needed

poetry, wanted to be at last a published toad,
not just another passing migrant, but one who'd
brought us, words and all, its precious load,

the secret jewel. There, between Marvell and Norman
MacCaig, it questioned the simile of a purse, probed our human
habit of shedding ourselves into books, and claimed common

descent as it climbed (Milton, Marianne Moore) further
from our imaginary garden and into another
gap where the prose romance begins. Malory's Arthur

hears Bufo croak the news of an epic to be written,
telling of the many royal skins it has worn then eaten,
in spawning strings of verse, *The Natterjacks of Britain*.

30

Two White Horses, chalk on their minds, argue
shades of grey. The distant one accepts the sugar
unwhinnyingly. Nothing ails this colt, eager

to please his master, yet he chafes at the old-fashioned bit
and knows the true word when it is whispered at
his untuned ear. He'd plunge right into a sheet

of blankness, despising bridges, to drink. He knows the cure
for anything slow. The other has seen it all before.
Rule breakers, hooves in a ditch, how they lure

foalhardiness to oblivion. He won't raise
his head, but can transfigure (like those pit ponies)
grass roots to a dream of hay. He'll spend his days

on a small pressed patch, apparently content, among
new turbines, old pylons, avoiding the young,
shaking his mane at the inconsiderate muck they've flung.

31

Dry sorrel, teasel, grasses flattened by the flood.
The faint beginnings of a gibbous moon. A tiny bird
crosses the path (last year's leaves and mud)

to the river, lower now, but still flowing at a pace.
The old sluice is making a noise, insists there's a race
to be run, though it was lost long ago by His Grace.

A well-dressed scarecrow's stretched-out arms pretend
to approach the US Army Air Force strip behind
the Folly, the ghost of a duchess watching him land.

All the world and its dog is out to mark the beginning
of the end of winter. The last of a peaceful day is shining
from the airfield, through the Eyecatcher, turning

its Restoration façade into a theatre set.
It was, indeed, the home of a pantomime cat,
when Boots owned the land. Now a holiday let.

32

The phone rings and, panic-stricken, you try to recall
things you've been doing this week so you can fill
those free minutes. You won't mention the hotel,

or weaving between its small tables to a specialist
in dementia, though this dream is what has moved you most.
Write down what you actually did, so it isn't lost:

Drove to St Neots for the sake of certain poetic forms.
Walked to the Folly. Checked the bedroom smoke alarms.
Sat and listened to Bruno Walter doing Brahms.

Ate vegan pastry. Drank a Christmas beer.
Walked to the old ford. Checked the drain was clear.
Sat and listened to Bernard Roberts' *Hammerklavier*.

Watched ten episodes of a Scandi noir
in Swedish with subtitles. Walked to the car.
Sat and listened to barking dogs and the tumble dryer.

33

Here they come again, crowding into my head,
those unknown recognisable ones, as if I had
met them somewhere. Are they my living dead?

No good saying it's just imagination, dream
feels so oddly true. One with our name
introduced herself the other night, the same

smile, almost, the same voice, but no one I knew.
Nor do I see why I must accept the accepted view
and unbelieve what instinct tells me, that we do

survive, as Donne believed, one short sleep past,
as all those mystical texts I used to read insist,
and Egypt, and the SPR. Tonight's cast

is preparing behind the curtain. Stage effects, sleight
of mind, the scientists laugh. And what else, they're right,
could it be? Head down. Put out the light.

34

You have to be a little bit unbalanced to write:
poplars leaning above the Kym that whisks a white
duck or paper cup to the bridge and out of sight.

You have to have something you are holding back
or attempting to suppress, a grief, an anger, a deep dark
resentment or dissatisfaction. The willows crack

as they are meant to do. But they shoot free of the break
in lines of three, and then into buds that will make
catkins and leaves and flowers. You have to be awake

when others are dreaming, and dream when others are out cold.
The waters, muddy, persistent, irresistible, hold
your life beneath the surface and will soon have sold

you down the river if you don't reach out for a reed,
a straw, an overhanging rush, a feather, tread
water and pull yourself up word by word.

35

It's true, he came from here, the inventor of the sandwich, filled
his time with politics (adding a spicy garnish), held
significant posts and an insignificant mistress, killed

in the foyer of the Royal Opera House – she could sing –
perhaps while he was ordering a snack, or did he bring
a packed supper for the two of them? It seems this fling

affected his judgement: soon he was a few slices short,
as they say in Huntingdon. Spare, then, a thought
for John, Fourth Earl of Sandwich, who is not

acclaimed as the patron of Cook, or named as Montagu of Breda,
but known for bread and beef, the eponymous fast food
that's gone round the world and now returns to brood

in his own small town, in Subway, Costa, Greggs,
where homeless Martha sings and John the squaddie begs
for change outside from a rough nest of sleeping bags.

36

The landline's dead. The water is off. A night of gales
across the leylandii's Onedin Line sails
above my wooden cabin. Now the electricity fails.

All morning I turn taps, press at switches
as if something will happen. Only a satellite watches
and advises via Twitter. The green rig lurches

towards sunrise. Suddenly, there's a shudder of power
in the fridge, a light flickers on, the midnight hour
flashes red, water pumps from the shower

in gasps and groans. Where have we arrived today?
A shore, strewn with cypress and birch, assault and affray
on the news. Aftermath. Post-mortem. Say

you were usurped and wrecked and found yourself here,
with courtiers, a daughter, a monster, a tame spirit of the air,
your own special arts, plus a Bible and Shakespeare.

37

A passing rat, a vole-shaped hole, and now this
in our humane trap. A trembling thing. No use
putting it in the garden, it will return, unless

I walk it down the lane to the bridge: a little water
clears us of such pests. Though we know there is a greater
threat down there beside the stream, a hater

of humanity and every sentimental tale
for children (Ratty or Dormouse), who knows full well
what you are thinking, the words you hum. The invisible

something you have dreamt waits here by the bridge,
and nothing you can do except walk on, and urge
your kids to be quick. Release the thing on to the verge

and watch it dart towards the river. Sing your way
home again capriccioso, to spend the day
in folderol and gruff riposte and childish play.

38

A friend from America emails, telling of wildfires
and White House fury. Curious relief that ours
is the soggiest, foggiest, least combustible of shires,

our *Bücherverbrennung* long since cold, grassed
over, a fading cropmark, a puritanical waste.
We're safe. And not to be cavalier, even the worst

would only provoke a shrug at this late date.
I think of my father: all those immaculate
rings made from the news laid so lovingly in the grate

for fifty years. I do the same. A poisonous wraith
of 2018 puffs from our Victorian hearth
as my reply to Santa Rosa takes a breath

to leap the gap between those sickly Wellingtonia
marching through our minor public school, and sequoia
standing up to whatever comes in California.

39

On the horizon the Nine Maidens are standing up
for equality, as well they might. They don't stop
to take a breath, but broadcast their agitprop

views on watts and tempest, why we shouldn't mine
and burn a deep and fossilised resource, when
power can be generated without a visible line

and naturally as leaves on a tree. Beneath real trees
Bunyan was here; then progress bought his pilgrim's lease
and hymns were swiftly turned to whispered conspiracies.

'My theme is carpe diem,' one says; then it's place,
clean air, empowerment, faith… The pylons hiss
bitterly, 'PC!' and down the lines it goes:

'Our nudes came through, we never closed,
just another windmill show, look at them, posed
motionless, tall and bare and white, signalling virtues.'

40

Our meeting place – the old police station and court,
a museum now, complete with cell – looks out
on Funerals, the resurrected Waterstones, a cut

through to Waitrose past the Weeping Ash, though
our one concern is with the words before us, how
the author got away with it, what does this show…

I read out stories, we discuss them, but we're dumb
as Quakers (each Sunday they are silent in this room)
at tales of how a visiting psychic's pendulum

swung by one April evening, catching their voices,
the dead who cannot leave – the girl who sends her kisses
to Passchendaele, the boy whose unresting place is

beside a giant abacus upstairs. He shakes
the beads as if they were the bars where his mistakes
still rattle freely, and the floor above us creaks.

41

Up the road, where Robert Cotton spins and weaves
a future British Library out of what survives
the wrecked monasteries, a group of men arrives.

Browsing, drinking, talking. One of them contemns
all authors not Ben Jonson, then storms
to bed, raging through himself all night, and dreams

of his boy, a child merely, in London, his small brow
cut red as if a sword gave the blow
and left him cross-marked like London's doors to show

plague within. Ben Jonson runs to his friend,
Camden, still up and reading, who'll surely understand,
a wise man, a teacher. He says it's a trick of the mind.

'Be not disjected, Ben.' But then the letters come
and Jonson reads the news of his first son, whom
we remember only for a little poem.

42

The winter night sky is still largely free
of light pollution, though at least one property
down the lane is trying its best to make us see

nothing but its own white clapboard views:
all we need to notice is its awesome size
and not, above its solar panels, the infinite ways

of creation, stars that measure top speed in years,
constellations performing to a county's frozen cars
glass-harmonica music of the absent spheres.

But they are only accompanying these winter owls
that warble to each other, their tawny mating calls
a concerto for dead trees. Galactic drum rolls

announce a final movement. Up on the gable
of the new house something will suddenly gleam, swivel
a big dish, peer into the invisible.

43

At Grafham Water, a group of fifty-somethings learning
to layer a hedge. 'We paid to do this!' says one of them, grinning
into the bitter wind as I admire their cunning

crewel work. Thirty yards a day the local hedgers
would have been told, back when such stakes and pleachers
(or were they 'stowels' here?) were wrought into barbed cages

to keep livestock out. Some straggly metres
are all this cheerful bunch have managed. Not that it matters
since the animals left. But it's a curious sight

as they stoop among snowfields, the teacher, the widow, the retired
financier (a hedge-fund manager, surely) who heard
the call on local radio for anyone prepared

to cut, twist, shape a windproof barrier against –
what? Time itself? Look how this cut bends
just enough to keep it alive, so the sap ascends.

44

Each time we came, the black peat had shrunk
a little and you had grown more. It makes me think
how childish we must have seemed striding the lode bank

on our clever stilts, tossing you bits of information:
your parents, not the peat, showing signs of regression
and no Holme Post to help with the measuring.

Now you've found a home in a different fen, drive
superconductive roads across the globe, your lives
no slow circular boardwalk. A thaw at last, so we've

returned with other snowbirds to that windpump waiting
for powers it can't use, for punt-guns and sedge-cutting,
will-o'-the wisp, Black Shuck. Someone is shooting

a scene in which it will all appear. No time to watch
wildlife on the mere, to pan from Adventurers' Fen to Reach.
Too cold, says the horizon. Quick march.

45

Muntjacs we expect, the dead badger, rodents trapped
and hung on a fence, but surely no tigers (except
Fen Tigers). Anything dangerous must have escaped

from the Legends of East Anglia. Turn right for Gidding,
however, you'll hear the truth, a dull note of foreboding
that sharpens as you pay and enter. Past the meerkats, padding

across the stage, there, look, the distinguished thing
Rousseau and Blake were out to capture and Hughes sang
a psalm to pacify. A tiger does not belong

in the Huntingdonshire wolds. Did it kill that keeper,
this vast creature slumped now in a snoring stupor?
Did you? No, let's not disturb the innocent sleeper.

Even those ginger stripes on our sofa (gentle beast
from a neighbouring void who strolled in, filled our days, most
loving to the hand) we leave alone in night's forest.

46

Poking air holes in the ice of our pond – streaks
of flattened reed, old false bulrush stalks –
I stir birdsong, dove-bubbles, left-wing croaks

from a right-wing crow. Spring can't quite commit
to sweet air – as sunflower seeds in a tube invite
the wood pigeon from the tip of a twig he can't quite

leave without looking silly. Windscreens are glazed
with Candlemas frost. The 7.30 sky's a haze
of waxing light. Someone appears to know the place

we hide our door key – that magpie. Mr Noon
scares it off with his nest of stories. In the *Guardian*
more shooting, but here the news is a pheasant's run

down the garden to find a loophole as if it knows
there'll be no gun control. The pond's frozen
over again. A pibroch is all our robin has.

47

The Damnation of Faust in my cold ears, I follow my nose
across this rutted field, just sufficiently frozen
to keep off the clay. In the company of Berlioz,

it doesn't seem so biting, though the wind's a keen
recommendation for hell. A transformation scene
reveals the folly, now the church spire alone

in bony *trompe l'oeil* of elder. Three shires
are stretched out before me. Thirty-five years
spent learning to tread those high-tension wires

from home to work and back with a poem, like that guy
who contemplated without terror the whole way
between the twin towers, just him, a pole and the sky.

Will-o'-the-wisps have danced, Hungarians marched past,
and soon the Ride to the Abyss. Don't walk too fast
back to your study. Think of Petit. Think of Faust.

48

Alone, I don't like what I find in the silence,
and don't like what I don't find, either: for instance
I know you have gone from me today no real distance

up the hill to Bedfordshire, where the other Johns
(Bunyan, Howard), ignored by a hundred flashing phones,
look greenly over your head to see if the prison's

reforming itself. It's not as if I'm in solitary.
I have the cat. I have Facebook friends. The olive tree
from Herts we bought as a kind of celebratory

merging of your Greek and my dendrophilia
is not bad company. Come back, though, will you.
I don't want to live alone. In fact, let's fill

this room as we did for our Egypt years, or as Poirot might
at the end of one of those Agatha Christies you delight
in reading cover to duvet every single night.

49

Up here is where Broadview wants to harvest wind
(of which the Urals ensure a surfeit), unconcerned
that it's also the base from which America chose to send

Flying Fortresses on bombing raids, that here marks
the place where some came back to stay. These concrete tracks
we use for jogging, walking the dog, riding our bikes,

were what they limped towards, their last approach
in line with the weathercock on the spire of St Andrew's Church,
whose bell today announces time. A sign in the porch

warns of incoming turbines. Think of history.
Think of natural beauty. No one mentions the mystery
of those helmeted aircrew on the tracks. It's just a story.

But we've known people who are clear what they have seen.
Yes, wind power is rational, economical, clean,
but there are other sources to tap, have always been.

50

We showed my mother the rings of Saturn and Jupiter's moons
through the telescope here on our patio once,
and have watched the space station hurtling over the fence

towards us. Orion. The Plough. Venus. And showers
of meteors. Leonids, Perseids. Ours
to watch for nothing – at least until the gated neighbours

decide it's a threat. I guess this is like Grovers Mill,
where Orson Welles's Martians landed (H.G. Wells
had left), where anything can happen, where long-distance calls

to the stars may or may not be answered. Gripped as I was
when young by books like *Flying Saucers – Serious Business*,
I joined BUFORA, would scan west London's skies,

discovering nothing but night flights from Heathrow.
I blame the Apollo missions, but *Star Trek* too,
which still invites us to split infinity, to boldly go.

51

Snowed in. Blizzards such as we've never seen.
The lane choked. The house clenched by a cold machine
that wants the truth from us. We won't give in.

Stay mute, deep in layers, gritting our teeth
as it goes for joints, nose, feet, our very breath,
then puts out a red warning. Yet up the path

comes smiling Mr Noon with news from the Pole
whose heatwave bred this rough beast. Now we can crawl
towards Brexit to be bored. Leaving's impossible.

I vote we make the best of things by staying here,
like Cromwell's statue in St Ives, a roundhead in a square,
pointing sternly at winter. It's not the Shrovetide Fair

stirs beneath that snowy hat, nor a memory of when
they kept chickens, their farm. Hard now, inhuman.
A rack turns in his head. It's Ireland once again.

52

Today is on. Yesterday, Brian Redhead
spoke as I was shaving. A single safety blade
that doubled, and now it's tripled. Mishal Husain has said

what May is going to say. But as for the times
I've faced this mirror, while miners tore at uniforms,
and radioactive rain fell on to farms,

and flower tributes grew outside the palace,
I couldn't say. Wiping my face, the stubborn whiteness,
I look for better news. It's March. Our month of grace,

the Greening equinox (there'll be no magic show
though the candles keep on lighting however hard you blow),
then May will speak. Instead of angels in the snow,

a riffling, a shuffling and dealing of bright new words
as if by the very daughter of Elysium. Outside, birds
fight over broken pieces of cake, their trump cards.

53

The Leiermann begins to turn his handle: still it falls,
snow on snow, as the poet said – before Holst
and Darke came walking across it with their carols.

That homeless summons from the whiteout strikes my tongue
and groove and leaves me glad I'm listening here among
the books, not out there trying to hold a song

against winter: a final drone, resolved, but barely,
then the silence of the snow. A single robin clearly
thinks there's something more to add, and whistles sourly

out of a box tree, shaking crystals down as he darts
in search of applause, and so the blackbird starts,
and then another, bird on bird. Who needs the arts

when nature is so heartfelt? No, old man,
you can't persuade me to donate, yet Schubert can
who summons angels even as he shakes the tin.

54

Thaw is also one of the gods, with strength enough
to shift this boulder of ice off the path, save
tender plants or peel the tarnished plating from a grave.

Unloved, yet he it is who brings some colour
into the negative, playing percussion solo
over its tedious white noise. You think he's shallow?

He'll quickly show you travellers just how deep
once it's the marching season. Out comes the harp
and soon you'll be in floods, begging him stop.

His fellow sprites and nymphs prepare guerrilla raids
in collaboration with the trolls of minor roads,
light-elves, heat-giants. He dampens reeds

for his grand finale. 'How they worship the works of the Queen,'
he tuts, 'but where is she?' Down a green lane,
by a fence, in the ditch, her grey head may be seen.

55

The forty-year calendar on my study window ledge
I brought from Cornwall for my daughter, who was the wrong age,
fourteen, I guess – since 2000 is where the gauge

begins, running through to 2039.
You keep it true each January, turning it on
so day, month, year (a leap year's red) align.

It's beech, I'd say, turned on a lathe, metal plates
set at the top, engraved with (apart from all the dates)
a ship's wheel, a clipper. Here in port it waits

for my attention. There, it's done at last, and it occurs
to me today on what would have been my late father's
ninety-fifth birthday: when the last year expires

and no brass is left on which to solemnly engrave
another date, an Arthurian barge, or the Jumblies' sieve,
I will or would or might be almost eighty-five.

56

Chaconne, a single violin against the world, performed
by Grumiaux the Magnificent: our universe tamed
for thirteen minutes, its circus act live-streamed

to this small hut in Huntingdonshire.
I listen, recalling the first fiddle piece I ever
played, on open strings: *A Toye*. This reverie

is enough to send me on my way. You'd think for once
I'd stay awake instead of going to join those clowns
inside my head. Didn't I feel eternity pounce

and gnaw at the bars of time? Now I'm making friends
in my dream with marching gladiators, while Belgian hands
craft their filigree, unheard. Though the music ends

Bach goes on pushing the Age of Reason to the edge
of reason, like a blade in Flag Fen, sacred, such
ingenuity and refinement, yet too deep to reach.

57

The Ouse has reached its limit. The church at Hemingford Grey,
for some reason perched on its bank, has nothing to say
that will keep the water down, though someone thought to lay

engineering bricks against a flood – not much
to hold back a force like that. We stand on the edge
and listen to Britain's oldest plane tree, huge

in its faded combats: *To survive, you must be slow.*
Three hundred winters could not bring me low.
Ask the church, the manor house, Green Knowe,

whose children... Ah, the children, yes, of course, the ones
by Lucy Boston. Chimneys? Something like that. Stones?
She started late – past sixty, according to our phones,

though none of us have read her. I stand with my sister,
reading the latest Ouse instead: this Thursday Adventure,
Down the Bright Stream, turning our pages faster.

58

Pronouncing it 'Cow' they pass his name (*Cowper? Dunno.*)
on a crawl from Cromwell's bar to the Pepys to the Barley Mow,
since variety's the spice of life. At least they know

a famous poet lived here: news that stays
on its plaque above the *Hunts Post* offices,
even as circulation decays. And if they praise

England, with all her faults, or move in a mysterious way
along that church wall, monarch of all they survey,
towards the cup that cheers… he's still the castaway

stranded inside the town's ring road, repeating
'God made the country' to these guys eating
chips on a sofa. Someone is always going to be writing

on poplars or an oak tree, signing suburban dusk
with answers to what their age hasn't thought to ask,
but will perhaps in a century or two, the unending task.

59

Two long-tailed tits tap the glass.
It could almost be a code – notification of loss
or warning of extinction. My father used to have to pass

so many tests in Morse. He was little more than eighteen.
His coming-of-age. By the time he reached twenty-one
he hardly needed a key. Both my parents are gone

with the code, as are their March birthdays, 4th and 5th.
Rhett and Scarlett brought the pair of them together.
At Cineworld, our elder daughter kisses her mother.

We're watching a film for Mother's Day: *Lady Bird*.
Nothing on the screen is as poignant as what I heard
trailed at my window. The promised biopic: a hoard

of hair, feathers, spider's webs and all they've scraped
from my lair, bits of biro, word fragments dropped,
salvaged, softly woven to a nest, bottle-shaped.

60

The power lines again, this time towards that farm
we used to walk the pushchair through. Still the same
woman who chased me off so angrily that time –

How'd I like to have a stranger invade my garden?
Though now she warbles by on three wheels, suddenly
veering off the pavement to the wrong side of the road,

and her husband… silhouetted there against the fields
as he was for stubble burning. A townee – I was told,
Get lost. I greeted him yesterday as he hobbled

to check the post, Prometheus receiving his final warning.
Power came when the war ended. We go on burning
our stubble, protecting our gardens, saying good morning

to people though we don't know who the hell we are.
Just keep on walking. Follow the final wire.
When it ends, warm both hands before the fire.

acknowledgements

'Huntingdonshire Codices' 15, 18, 28, 34, 38, 49 and 56 were included separately in *The Interpretation of Owls: Selected Poems 1977–2022* (ed. Kevin Gardner), published by Baylor University Press in March 2023. Some have also appeared in: *Acumen* (53, 56, 57), *Agenda* (17, 23, 44), *Anthropocene* (49), *Brittle Star* (47, 48), *Critical Survey* (31, 35), *Fenland Poetry Journal* (4, 5, 25, 37, 41, 42), *Long Poem Magazine* (6, 8, 10, 11, 12, 50, 51), *Magma* (24), *The Poetry Review* (32, 33, 34, 36), *Poetry Salzburg Review* (16, 27, 29, 40), *Quadrant* (28, 30, 55), *Stand Magazine* (7, 9) and *Wild Court* (18, 19, 20).

about the poet

John Greening is recipient of several major prizes and a Cholmondeley Award. Beyond the many collections represented in *The Interpretation of Owls: Selected Poems 1977–2022* (ed. Gardner, Baylor University Press, 2023), he has produced anthologies and editions of major poets. Having lived in London, Egypt, Scotland and New Jersey, he and his wife settled in East Anglia, where their two daughters grew up.

JOHNGREENING.CO.UK 🌐 🐦 @GREENINGPOET